NO ONE
Wants to Play with Me!

Story and Photography
by
Patty J. Keith

> A special "Thank You" to Carson and Carley Wright,
>
> my youngest editors and granddaughters, who ensure that every word in
>
> the Duck Ponder Series is child friendly and for always believing in happy endings.
>
> For you and God's glory, I write each word.
>
> P.J.K.

Copyright © 2015 Patty Keith

No part of this publication may be reproduced in any form without the written permission of the author and publisher.

All rights reserved

Dandelion graphics by Brent Alan Wright 2013
Original oil art by Suzanne Gaudette Way, copyright 2011

Scriptures taken from the Holy Bible, New International Version®, NIV®. Copyright © 1973, 1978, 1984, 2011 by Biblica, Inc.™ Used by permission of Zondervan. All rights reserved worldwide. www.zondervan.com The "NIV" and "New International Version" are trademarks registered in the United States Patent and Trademark Office by Biblica, Inc.™

Scripture taken from the Modern English Version copyright © 2014 by Military Bible Association. Used by permission. All rights reserved.

Scripture quotations are from The Holy Bible, English Standard Version® (ESV®), copyright © 2001 by Crossway, a publishing ministry of Good News Publishers. Used by permission. All rights reserved.

PRINTED IN THE UNITED STATES OF AMERICA

Duck Ponder Series: Book VII , ISBN: 978-0-9893303-5-0

"Miserable Marty" is a nickname that Marty the male Mallard maintains because he stays mad, mopey or moody most of the time.

Miserable Marty does not look very happy, does he?

Marty is Miserable!

Miserable Marty does not have many friends because he does not know how to be a friend to others.

A man that hath friends must show himself friendly:
Proverbs 18:24 (MEV)

"Come on Jack. Let's get out of here before Miserable Marty catches up to us," Thelma whispered.

Ponder this:
Mallard Ducks may waddle along slowly, but they can fly pretty fast. At top speed they can hit 70 miles per hour!

Thelma and Jack quietly waddled away from Miserable Marty as fast as they could because they did not want to be his friend either.

Remembering that the bible says we should always be kind to one another,

Ref: (Ephesians 4:32)

Jack decided to stop and wait for Marty.

But Marty was so miserable he just waddled right past Jack.

"Hey Marty, wait up! What's the matter" Jack asked.

"No one wants to play with me," Marty sulked.

Jesus said that we should treat others the way we would want to be treated.
Ref: (Luke 6:31-36)
That is not always an easy thing to do with Miserable Marty.

"I am going home! I don't have any friends. Everyone is always so mean to me!!" Marty began to whine.

"Wait just a minute Marty. Are you sure about that?" Jack questioned him.

Thelma saw that Jack was obeying God by being kind to Miserable Marty.

Thelma wanted to please God too, so she joined them. But Chester limped away before anyone could notice.

"Why do you think no one wants to play with you," Jack asked Miserable Marty.

Miserable Marty began to tell his story....

"First, Walker said he would play Hide and Seek with me but...

that was **not** what I wanted to play. SO I got mad at him!"

"While he was hiding I went to find someone else who would play what I wanted to play," Marty complained.

"Soon I found Hank and Henrietta,
but I only wanted to play with Hank.
I did not want to play with Henrietta.

When I told Hank **only he could be my friend**, they both swam away from me as fast as they could," Marty continued.

By then Walker had quit hiding and agreed to play chase like I wanted, but he would not let me go first, so I **yelled** at him and said, "That's not fair!"

I want to go first Walker. That's not fair!

"When Walker started chasing me anyway I got **mad** at him and flew out of the water"

Ponder this: Mallards can fly nearly vertical, if needed. This includes taking off from the water almost straight up. Pekin Ducks can not fly.

"I don't like playing with Pekin ducks anyway," Marty grumbled out loud.

Ref: (Proverbs 18:21)

"Did Marty just say he doesn't like playing with me? Jack questioned

Do you think Marty's words hurt Jack's feelings?

"Soon I found 4 drakes playing together. I decided to join them. But there were already 2 drakes on each team and I made the teams uneven.
The other drakes told me I would have to wait until the next game to play.

I don't want to wait for my turn. I want to play now!

So I broke the line and got in front of Melvin."

"Melvin did not like me breaking line. He chased me away and told me not to come back until I wanted to play fair."

Jack realized that Marty did not understand how God wants us to love others more than ourselves.

Ref: (Philippians 2:3-11)

So Jack listened patiently until Miserable Marty had stopped moaning.

Jack wanted to share God's gift with Marty in hope that he would no longer be miserable.

You were taught, with regard to your former way of life, to put off your old self, which is being corrupted by its deceitful desires; to be made new in the attitude of your minds; and to put on the new self, created to be like God in true righteousness and holiness. Ephesians 4:22-24 (NIV)

Miserable Marty was ready for some good news so he swam closer to Jack and Thelma to listen.

"God wants you to have lots of friends. He wants you to be happy. Only you can decide if you will obey God. Obeying God means bearing His good fruit to others," Jack explained.

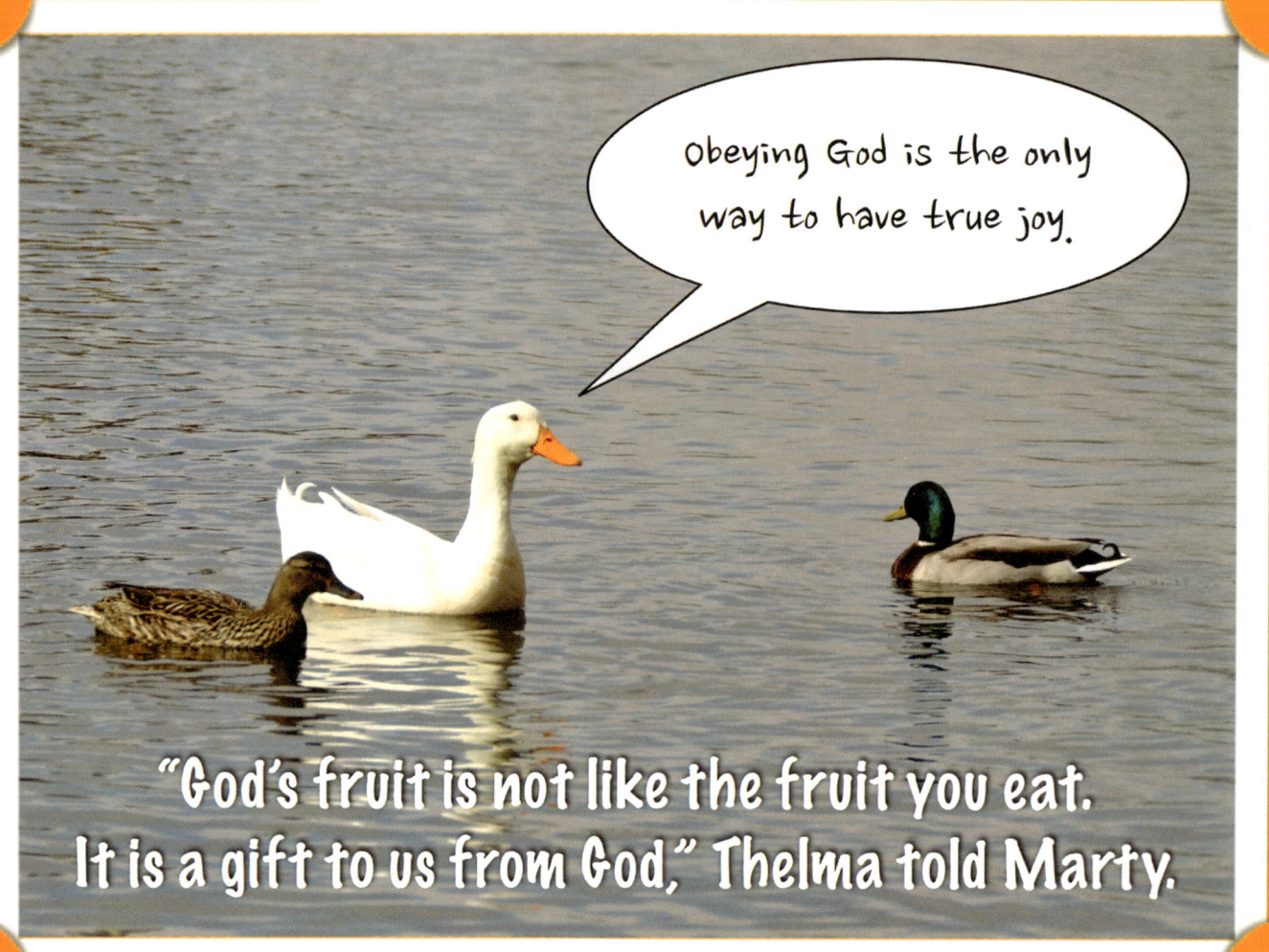

Obeying God is the only way to have true joy.

"God's fruit is not like the fruit you eat. It is a gift to us from God," Thelma told Marty.

"Tell me about the fruit of God's spirit.

I want to obey God."

"Can you ever forgive me for hurting your feelings Henrietta?" Marty begged.

Hank and Walker forgave Marty first.
Then Henrietta forgave Marty too.

After all the Mallards forgave him, Marty realized that he had always had lots of friends that would play with him.

<u>Marty was the problem.</u>

He just needed to learn how to be a better friend.

Get rid of all bitterness, rage and anger, brawling and slander, along with every form of malice.

Ephesians 4:31 (NIV)

Thank you God for your gift of a gentle spirit and for always forgiving me when I misbehave.

The End

Quack with JACK

1. Is the fruit of the Spirit a coconut or an orange or a banana?

2. How many of the Spirit's fruit can you name?

3. Do you think you will play better with your friends when you bear the fruit of God's Spirit?

Will you choose to have a good day or a bad day? God gives YOU that choice.

Be sure to read all the books in the Duck Ponder Series:

Book I

Will You be My Friend? (even IF I am different from you)

Book II

I Wish I was a Mallard...but God made me a Pekin instead

Book III - Hank the Honking Goose Learns to Listen

Book IV - Never FEAR! God is (always) near

Book V - Bully Be Gone!

Book VI - It is NOT Okay to Disobey

Book VII - No One wants to Play with Me!

Book VIII - Do I look Adopted to You?

Coming Soon - The Secret we are all dying to know

CPSIA information can be obtained
at www.ICGtesting.com
Printed in the USA
LVIC04n0124170316
479519LV00004B/12